# JOURNAL

## INSPIRATIONAL PROMPTS FOR CHRISTIAN TEEN GIRLS

Melanie Redd

ROCKRIDGE
PRESS

For general information on our other products and services or to obtain technical support, please contact our Customer Care Department within the United States at (866) 744-2665, or outside the United States at (510) 253-0500.

Rockridge Press publishes its books in a variety of electronic and print formats. Some content that appears in print may not be available in electronic books, and vice versa.

TRADEMARKS: Rockridge Press and the Rockridge Press logo are trademarks or registered trademarks of Callisto Media Inc. and/or its affiliates, in the United States and other countries, and may not be used without written permission. All other trademarks are the property of their respective owners. Rockridge Press is not associated with any product or vendor mentioned in this book.

Interior and Cover Designer: Rachel Haeseker
Art Producer: Meg Baggott
Editor: Carolyn Abate
Production Editor: Emily Sheehan
Production Manager: Jose Olivera

Illustration © Myriam Van Neste
Author photo courtesy of Emily Redd

Scripture quotations marked (NIV) are taken from the Holy Bible, New International Version®, NIV®. Copyright © 1973, 1978, 1984, 2011 by Biblica, Inc.™ Used by permission of Zondervan. All rights reserved worldwide. www.zondervan.com. The "NIV" and "New International Version" are trademarks registered in the United States Patent and Trademark Office by Biblica, Inc.™

ISBN: Print 978-1-64876-801-9

R0

# HOW TO USE THIS JOURNAL

Welcome to *Live in Light: Inspirational Prompts for Christian Teen Girls.*

I am so glad you've picked up this book!

We have designed this book with so many features that we hope will add to your personal devotional and reflection times. There are quizzes, chances to draw, checklists, assessments, stories, personal examples, and so much more.

It is also my hope that you will be greatly encouraged over the coming weeks as you read, write, study, and pray. The Bible is a powerful book, and I believe that you will experience much hope, victory, and joy as you spend devotional time with the Lord each day.

For the teen girl who wants to grow closer to the Lord, this is a wonderful and easy-to-use resource that can be readily incorporated into your daily life. The book is organized for you to achieve maximum spiritual growth in a minimum amount of time.

**Daily Verses:** This book offers a thoughtfully and carefully selected collection of verses from the Bible to offer you wisdom, direction, and encouragement.

**Daily Prompts:** Following the daily verses are short devotions, writing prompts, and questions to lead you as you pray over, consider, and apply the scripture you have read for that particular day.

**Daily Reflections:** After you've read the Bible verses and considered the daily prompts, write down your thoughts and ideas. Take a few minutes to interact with the truths that you have read and jot down your responses. Some will invite you to creatively share your ideas, make lists, draw pictures, or illustrate your dreams. This step can be life-altering!

**Weekly Reflections:** At the conclusion of each week, you will have the opportunity to go back over the following week and make observations. You'll consider what you learned, the things you journaled, and some of the lessons God is teaching you.

practical wisdom, this book offers daily hope to counteract the challenges you encounter.

This book will be especially helpful to you if:

✗ *You'd love to gain more wisdom and insights into life and decision-making.*

✗ *You need insights in how to pray.*

✗ *You want better friendships and relationships.*

✗ *You'd like to have a greater impact on those around you.*

✗ *You'd like to have more joy.*

✗ *You'd like to know more about God's plans for your future.*

✗ *You are struggling to forgive someone.*

✗ *You want to really understand how amazing you are!*

✗ *You'd like to grow closer to God.*

Truly, this book has been specially designed with you in mind. Each devotional, verse, and writing prompt has been prayed over and carefully created for you to use. My prayer is that you will be so encouraged, uplifted, and inspired as you read, study, ponder, and journal your ideas and responses. Specifically, I am praying Ephesians 1:17–19 from the Message Bible for you:

> *"I ask—ask the God of our Master, Jesus Christ, the God of glory—to make you intelligent and discerning in knowing him personally, your eyes focused and clear, so that you can see exactly what it is he is calling you to do, grasp the immensity of this glorious way of life he has for his followers, oh, the utter extravagance of his work in us who trust him—endless energy, boundless strength!"*

God has amazing plans for your life! He adores you, and he wants to use you in a mighty way. Let's start this journey together. . . .

MELANIE

# INTRODUCTION

Let's face it—today's teens face pressures as never before. Whether you are trying to take your team to the playoffs, your band to the championships, or your grades to the honor roll, you probably feel pressure to perform and do well. This can come from parents, youth pastors, teachers, coaches, peers, and society in general. It's a lot. Being a godly girl in this crazy world can sometimes feel impossible!

Your mom, grandmothers, aunts, and female mentors faced challenges as they were growing up, too. But today so many factors make it even more difficult to wholeheartedly follow Christ as a young woman. Your mom or grandma never had to worry about Snapchat or Instagram. Let's face it, navigating social media can be stressful. It can get you wondering, *Did anyone like my post? Do I have as many followers as my friends? Do I look fat in that picture? Am I enough?* It's a challenge to feel good about yourself with so much social comparison.

As if the notifications on your phone aren't enough to cause you anxiety, you may struggle with feelings of fear, worry, and uncertainty about the future. The weight of this world may be crushing down on you right now. You may also be facing difficult situations in your church, at work, or in your neighborhood. Perhaps your pastor has just left your church. Maybe you work and worship with some people who are really hard to get along with. You may even be dealing with something that no one else knows about—at home, with a friend, or in your own thought life.

Whatever is pressing in on you, there is always hope! This little book was created to encourage you with days and days of hope. The journal prompts that follow will help you seek God's wisdom as you face the world around you. You'll learn to better handle the pressures of social media, friends, boys, and even the adults in your life.

You'll be encouraged to journal, pray, and meditate on uplifting truths and inspiration from God's Word that will give you much hope and peace. You'll be able to find encouragement no matter what you are facing at the moment. Using the truth of the Bible, short stories, personal examples, and lots of

This book is dedicated to all of the amazing girls out there who want to take their spiritual journey to the next level.

You've chosen the best way . . . by falling in love with Jesus now and continuing to pursue and enjoy your relationship with him for the rest of your life.

I pray that you will grasp how much God loves you, find your identity completely in him, live boldly and courageously, and make a huge impact on this planet for the Lord!

**Areas of Study:** This book offers a variety of topics selected just for teen girls and their spiritual growth—things you can really relate to:

- Dealing with the challenges that life brings—difficult people, mean girls, peer pressure, social media, dating, and social issues.

- Dealing with your own emotions—fear, insecurity, loneliness, feeling left out, temptation, anxiety, self-doubt, and jealousy.

- Your mission—what does God have planned for you? How can he use you? How can you make a difference in this world? Is there hope for the future?

- Your relationships with people—friends, boys or girls, teachers, authority figures, parents, grandparents, and siblings.

- Your relationship with God—enjoying his love, finding his will, resting in his peace, learning to pray, reading the Bible, growing spiritually, and discovering more about his purpose for your life.

These topics and many more are interspersed throughout the journal. Today is a great day for you to begin! Turn the page, grab your favorite pen or pencil, and get started.

# HOW'S YOUR BALANCE?

"There is a time for everything, and a season for every activity under the heavens."
-ECCLESIASTES 3:1

It's easy to get stressed out when life feels overwhelming. Pressure can come from many directions—school, home, friends, your teammates, your community, social media. Use this space to identify and write about the pressures you feel. Remember, your writing is a safe conversation between you and God!

# GOD KNOWS YOUR LOCATION

"So then, each of us will give an account of ourselves to God."
-ROMANS 14:12

God knows about your choices—the things that consume your thoughts. How does this make you feel? As you start your day, take a few moments and write down everything you want to do today. When you're finished, go back to your list and ask God to give you his strength and his blessings as you seek to complete each task.

# HANDLE AUTHORITY LIKE A PRO

"Have confidence in your leaders and submit to their authority, because they keep watch over you as those who must give an account. Do this so that their work will be a joy, not a burden, for that would be of no benefit to you."

-HEBREWS 13:17

As a teen, I worked at a restaurant with a difficult boss who was hard to respect. I eventually learned that if I did my work without engaging in conflict, it made work less stressful. The Bible teaches us to submit to our authorities, because they keep watch over and often care for us, but it's not always easy. Think about three authority figures in your life right now: parents, teachers, coaches, or even a boss. Think about what it must be like to walk in their shoes. Write down five ways you can show them more compassion and kindness.

# CALL ON GOD

"Call to me and I will answer you and tell you great
and unsearchable things you do not know."

-JEREMIAH 33:3

The Bible tells us that we can call on God at any time and talk to him about anything. If you could meet him at Starbucks, what would your conversation entail? If you were sitting across from him over an iced latte or matcha, what would you say? Write down your words, then read the outline to him.

# THE PAIN OF REJECTION

"He was despised and rejected by mankind, a man of suffering, and familiar with pain. Like one from whom people hid their faces he was despised, and we held him in low esteem."

-ISAIAH 53:3

It's hard to believe that Jesus was rejected, hurt, ridiculed, and hated by the people in his day. You'd think his teachings of healing and helping would've made him the most popular guy on the planet, but that wasn't the case. Have you ever felt the sting of rejection? Maybe you didn't make the team you wanted or weren't invited to an important party? Write about your experience here. When you're finished, read back over your words. Remember that no matter how others treat you, Jesus loves you and will never leave you.

# YOU ARE WONDERFULLY MADE

"For you created my inmost being; you knit me together in my mother's womb. I praise you because I am fearfully and wonderfully made; your works are wonderful; I know it full well."

-PSALM 139:13–14

You are the only YOU on the planet! You are an original created by Almighty God—the most fabulous designer in the universe—so celebrate how amazing you are. Write down 10 talents, skills, or gifts that make you special. For example, you may be compassionate, funny, an excellent coder, a natural leader, good at playing the flute, or a great jump shooter. Don't be shy about singing your praises!

# SET BOUNDARIES

"Do not move your neighbor's boundary stone set up by your predecessors in the inheritance you receive in the land the Lord your God is giving you to possess."

-DEUTERONOMY 19:14

We have a tall fence around our backyard because we have a pool. It gives us an added measure of safety. We also need fences in our lives. They help us set boundaries for our emotions and our actions when they feel out of control, both in relationships and with ourselves. Think about setting up some boundaries in your life, with your time, and in your relationships. How would some sturdy "fences" improve your life?

# WEEKLY REFLECTION

For our first week together, we reflected on finding balance. I asked you to talk to Jesus like he was a friend at Starbucks and to share your feelings about the pain of rejection, among other topics. Which prompt stood out to you the most? Why do you think you were drawn to it, in particular? What do you think God may be trying to tell you?

# DO GOOD TO OTHERS

"Do not withhold good from those to whom it is
due, when it is in your power to act."

-PROVERBS 3:27

Doing nice things for others is powerful. It is an amazing experience that can make you feel good, as well. I'd like you to take inventory today and think of who you can help in your circle. It could be friends, family, teachers, coworkers, or teammates. Write down three names. Brainstorm one nice thing you could do for each of them this week—such as send a supportive text or email, deliver a batch of homemade cookies, wash their car, or buy them a coffee.

# CHECK YOUR ANGER

"In your anger do not sin. Do not let the sun go down while you are still angry, and do not give the devil a foothold."

-EPHESIANS 4:26–27

Lots of things can trigger anger, hurt, or frustration—arguing with siblings, being left out by friends, pressure from parents. Anger is not a sin, but anger can cause us to sin. To help you cope, create a few "anger prevention tactics." These are simple steps, such as praying, taking deep breaths, taking a walk—or even writing in your journal. Complete this thought: *If someone or something makes me really mad, I will do these things before I react.*

# GOD ANSWERS EVERY PRAYER (SERIOUSLY)

" . . . and she said to him, 'Pardon me, my Lord. As surely as you live, I am
the woman who stood here beside you praying to the Lord. I prayed for
this child, and the Lord has granted me what I asked of him.' "

-1 SAMUEL 1:26–27

I'm a person who prays about everything: family, friendships, finances, my job,
good health, and sometimes the weather. What do you pray about? Do you ask
God for help with grades, fears, loneliness, or wanting to make the team? Make
a prayer request page in the space below. Be specific so you will know when he
answers. Thank him for how he is going to answer your prayers.

# BE COMMITTED

"And may your hearts be fully committed to the LORD our God, to
live by his decrees and obey his commands, as at this time."

-1 KINGS 8:61

Think about the biggest commitments in your life. A club? A team? Church?
Family? Now, list the five things that take up most of your time or energy. Then,
go back over each one and ask yourself: *Is this something I'm passionate about?*
*Why am I doing it? Is this something I'd like to stay committed to? Does God have*
*something better for me to focus on?*

# DEALING WITH DISAPPOINTMENT

"Because he turned his ear to me, I will call on him as long as I live."
-PSALM 116:2

I was 16, and the boy I was dating started paying attention to one of my best friends. One day, he dumped me to start dating her. I was so hurt and disappointed by both of them. Unfortunately, disappointment is a part of life. Maybe you didn't make the cut for a team, get attention from someone you like, or get to buy that new outfit you so desperately wanted. Take a few moments and describe what happened the last time you felt deeply disappointed. Remember that God always hears us and gives us hope.

# HONOR YOUR PARENTS

"Honor your father and your mother, so that you may live
long in the land the Lord your God is giving you."

-EXODUS 20:12

The Bible tells us to honor our parents, even if we argue with them sometimes
or feel like they don't always understand. Draw a picture of your parents,
grandparents, an aunt or uncle, a foster parent—whoever is in charge in your
home. Try to come up with three things you appreciate about each person and
list them beside each picture. You may like your aunt's sense of humor or your
dad's enchiladas. Maybe you and your grandfather share a love of goofy sitcoms.
If you are willing, tell them what you wrote.

# SURROUNDED BY GOD'S LOVE

"May your unfailing love be with us, Lord, even as we put our hope in you."
-PSALM 33:22

Have you ever gotten an encouraging text at just the moment when you were feeling down? Perhaps the perfect song came on the radio at the same time you were thinking about a fun night with your friends. That was God speaking. He was showing you how much he loves you. Think about how God's love speaks to you and write about how this makes you feel.

# WEEKLY REFLECTION

This past week, feelings of anger and passion were front and center. We also discussed how God really, truly answers prayers. Which devotion from this week was your favorite? Which one did you not care for? Think about these two prompts and then explain here a bit more what you think it all means—what is God trying to teach you? What have you learned from your different reactions?

# DISCOVER HIS FAVOR

"May the favor of the Lord our God rest on us; establish the work
of our hands for us—yes, establish the work of our hands."

-PSALM 90:17

God's favor is a wonderful combination of grace, blessings, kindness, and love.
It's a safe home, a supportive teacher, a loyal friend, God's salvation. Take a
moment to think about the ways he has blessed you and your family, and list
them. Thank God for his goodness and tell him how much you appreciate
these things.

# HANDLING ANXIETY

"Do not be anxious about anything, but in every situation, by prayer and petition, with thanksgiving, present your requests to God. And the peace of God, which transcends all understanding, will guard your hearts and your minds in Christ Jesus."

-PHILIPPIANS 4:6–7

Anxiety and fear are strong emotions that so many young people face today. There is no shame in being afraid or nervous. However, the Bible tells us not to live anxious lives. How do you overcome your fears? How do you conquer anxiety? One of your greatest weapons is honest prayer. God tells us that when we open our hearts in prayer, he will flood our lives with amazing peace. Sharing with God how you really feel or how you struggle is important for healing. What might this peace look and feel like in your life?

# EXTENDING THE HAND OF FRIENDSHIP

"Therefore, as God's chosen people, holy and dearly loved, clothe your-
selves with compassion, kindness, humility, gentleness, and patience."

-COLOSSIANS 3:12

It's never fun to feel like you're on the outside. On the other hand, when
someone makes an effort to be your friend, it's awesome! Do you make an effort
to be inclusive with people who look or act differently than you? Think about
how you can be more friendly and more inclusive.

# MERCY: GIVE SOME, GET SOME

"Be merciful, just as your Father is merciful."
-LUKE 6:36

Mercy is the quality of being kind and compassionate to others, no matter how they act toward you. In the space provided, write down the names of your five best friends. Think about which person is the most merciful and which person is the least. Think about where you fit on this list. How does that make you feel? Close your devotional time by praying and asking God to make you full of mercy—just like him.

# THE STRENGTH TO KEEP GOING

"I have fought the good fight, I have finished the race, I have kept the faith."
-2 TIMOTHY 4:7

Life is full of races. For people your age, those "races" usually come in the forms of class projects and assignments. Some are much easier than others. What's one of the most challenging projects or assignments you've had to complete in your life? What made it hard? How did you get through it? Detail this experience from start to finish. What did you learn, and how can this help you with your next difficult assignment?

# RESPECT FOR ALL

"Show proper respect to everyone, love the family of
believers, fear God, honor the emperor."

-1 PETER 2:17

Most teens have someone that they really admire—a teacher, a coach, a friend,
even a YouTube personality. Make a list of three people who you really look up
to and respect. Next to each name, write down a few reasons why you admire
that person. As you conclude your devotional time, ask God to build the same
qualities into your life. Invite him to make you the kind of woman that others
will greatly respect.

# THERE'S NO SUCH THING AS "PERFECT"

"So God created mankind in his own image, in the image of God he created them; male and female he created them."

-GENESIS 1:27

Take a minute to think about how you feel about yourself, both the way that God created you and what you wish was different. Write down three to four things that you would call your "flaws." For example, maybe you don't like being the tallest girl in your class, or you're very shy. Pray about each one and invite him to show you how this quality is actually a perfect part of who you were created to be. God may have made you taller than most of the other girls, so you can spike a volleyball. Maybe you are quiet, but a great listener and supportive friend.

# WEEKLY REFLECTION

Several of the devotions over the past week were about your relationships with yourself and with others. Some of your relationships may be really solid, whereas others may need more attention. Choose one relationship from the following list that you'd like to focus on. Write about how you might be able to improve it.

- ✖ Your relationship with God
- ✖ Your relationship with your parents
- ✖ Your relationships with your brothers and sisters
- ✖ Your relationships with your best friends
- ✖ Your relationships with your teachers and coaches
- ✖ Other relationships

# GOD KNOWS YOUR PURPOSE

"The Lord will vindicate me; your love, Lord, endures forever—do not abandon the works of your hands."

-PSALM 138:8

Let's dream a little today. What are some of your goals, dreams, hopes, and ambitions? Is there a specific college you want to attend? Perhaps you want to travel to another country, write a book, start a business, or launch a podcast? Think about the next year, five years, or ten years. What are you looking forward to? Draw three images that best exemplify your biggest dreams. When you're finished, go back over each one and ask God to bless you. He wants to accomplish in and through your life.

# CAUTION SIGNS

"Be very careful, then, how you live—not as unwise but as wise, making the most of every opportunity, because the days are evil. Therefore do not be foolish, but understand what the Lord's will is. Do not get drunk on wine, which leads to debauchery. Instead, be filled with the Spirit."

-EPHESIANS 5:15–18

As a teen girl, you are going to have a lot of opportunities to make decisions—life-altering decisions. Who will you hang out with? What will you put in your body? Will you smoke, drink alcohol, or try drugs? If you like someone romantically, what types of actions and activity would you engage in? To help you make wiser choices, create a list of questions you will consider before making a big-life decision. For example: *How will this opportunity benefit me? How might it hurt me? Will it help anyone else? Will it hurt anyone else?*

# TRUST IN GOD

"Those who know your name trust in you, for you, Lord,
have never forsaken those who seek you."

-PSALM 9:10

God is trustworthy. We know this because the Bible tells us it's true, but we also learn it from experience. Consider the difficult experiences you had in your life, up until now. Think about the prayers that he answered. Were you able to avoid a dangerous situation, work out a misunderstanding with your bestie, or resolve a conflict with your parents? How has God shown up for you?

# SEEK WISDOM

"Do not forsake wisdom, and she will protect you; love her, and she will watch over you. The beginning of wisdom is this: Get wisdom. Though it cost all you have, get understanding."

-PROVERBS 4:6–7

Jess is one of the wisest young women I know. She is always learning, and often seeks the opinions of older, wiser friends in her life. She is truly a wise teenager. What are some other ways that you can identify other teens who are insightful, smart, and savvy? Complete this thought: When I think of a wise teenager, I think of . . .

_____

_____

_____

_____

_____

_____

_____

_____

_____

_____

_____

_____

_____

# CHURCH IS A VERB

"Every day they continued to meet together in the temple courts. They broke bread in their homes and ate together with glad and sincere hearts, praising God and enjoying the favor of all the people. And the Lord added to their number daily those who were being saved."

-ACTS 2:46–47

Churches were important to the early Christians, and they are still a part of our spiritual life today. Time spent in church draws us closer to God, connects us with other believers, and allows us to use our gifts. Think for a moment about your church (or a church you'd like to attend). What does it look like? What do you love about it? Draw a picture of your church. Then, add a few details about this church—the people, activities, mission, ministries, music, Bible study, pastors, and anything else you want to share.

# KINDNESS TO THOSE WHO HURT US

> "Be kind and compassionate to one another, forgiving each other, just as in Christ God forgave you."
>
> -EPHESIANS 4:32

It's easy to be kind to those who are kind to us. But how are we supposed to act when someone is, well, kind of a jerk? The Bible tells us to forgive them and show them compassion, too. This is very hard to do, but it is possible. As you think about your relationships today, does anyone come to mind who has hurt you or been mean to you? As difficult as it may be, write out a prayer expressing your hurt, pain, or anger, and how you'd like to forgive them. Invite God to help you really let this person and this pain go.

# A BEAUTIFUL HEART

"Charm is deceptive, and beauty is fleeting; but a
woman who fears the LORD is to be praised."

-PROVERBS 31:30

The Bible tells us that charm and beauty don't last forever, but a woman who deeply loves and respects God will be honored and praised. Describe your idea of a godly woman. Where does her beauty come from? How does she act? When you think of the most godly women you know, what do you think of?

# WEEKLY REFLECTION

Over the last seven days, your devotions covered making good decisions, trusting God, and growing closer to him. As you look back over your journal entries, how do you think you are learning to trust God more? How is your faith increasing? How are you becoming more courageous? Share your thoughts.

# NOT JUST ANOTHER BOOK

"Keep this Book of the Law always on your lips; meditate on
it day and night, so that you may be careful to do everything
written in it. Then you will be prosperous and successful."

-JOSHUA 1:8

The Bible is not just any book. It's a powerful guide for your life. Those who
read and meditate on it are promised great blessings. So, what can you do to
spend more time focusing on God's Word? Take a few minutes and list six or
seven ways you can make the Bible a bigger deal in your life. Then, complete
this thought: *If I were to spend 15 more minutes a day with my Bible, I think . . .*

# KINDNESS IS ITS OWN REWARD

"Whoever is kind to the poor lends to the LORD, and he
will reward them for what they have done."

-PROVERBS 19:17

Kindness. It prompts us to be generous. It leads us to give. It inspires us to care.
God promises to reward our kindness. So, what does kindness look like in your
little corner of the world? Who does a good job of modeling kindness: your best
friends, your parents, a teacher, your favorite aunt? Consider those around you
and ask where you see generosity and kindness taking place. Complete this
sentence: *When I think of kindness, I think of . . .*

# PREPARED IN ADVANCE

"For we are God's handiwork, created in Christ Jesus to do good works, which God prepared in advance for us to do."

-EPHESIANS 2:10

Let's do a personal inventory today. In the space provided, carefully consider and answer each of these questions:

1. What do you think God is preparing you to do in the future?
2. What do you believe you are specially created to do?
3. What are some of your greatest talents?
4. What things come easily for you?
5. What makes you unique and special?
6. What could you see yourself doing after college?
7. What are you most looking forward to for your future?

Once you have answered these questions, read back over your responses. Do you see any patterns or common themes? Be assured: God has amazing plans ahead for your life!

# BUILDING BRIDGES

*"If it is possible, as far as it depends on you, live at peace with everyone."*
-ROMANS 12:18

Have you ever taken the time to make something—paint a self-portrait, sew a piece of clothing, put together a scrapbook, or even create a TikTok dance? I bet you had to pay attention to a number of details to get everything just right. Your relationships also need our time and attention. Take a close look at your family members and friends. Is there anyone you find really challenging or hard to get along with? How can you build a better relationship with this person? Write down your thoughts.

_____

_____

_____

_____

_____

_____

_____

_____

_____

_____

_____

_____

# HOW'S YOUR MINDSET?

"Finally, brothers and sisters, whatever is true, whatever is noble, whatever is right, whatever is pure, whatever is lovely, whatever is admirable—if anything is excellent or praiseworthy—think about such things."

-PHILIPPIANS 4:8

Typically, there are two types of people: those who see the glass as half full and those who see it as half empty. The way we think and see life is a choice. Each day, we get to wake up and focus on the things we decide are imporant. The Bible encourages us to focus our thoughts on things that are true, pure, lovely, and admirable. But how do we do this? Finish this sentence: *To focus my mind and attention on better things, I need to . . .*

# FEELING CRUSHED

"We are hard pressed on every side, but not crushed; perplexed, but not in despair; persecuted, but not abandoned; struck down, but not destroyed."

-2 CORINTHIANS 4:8–9

If your family is like most families, you all hate to take out the garbage. In fact, you probably spend a lot of time mashing the trash down in the can so it doesn't need to be emptied. Sometimes our lives can feel a little like that garbage can, with things crushing down on us. Have you felt pressure like that? If your BFF were to ask you how you survive the days when you feel that way, what would you say to them?

# BROTHERS AND SISTERS

"Bear with each other and forgive one another if any of you has a grievance against someone. Forgive as the Lord forgave you."

-COLOSSIANS 3:13

Some of the most challenging things in life come in the form of our interactions with other people—people who hurt us, offend us, and just plain get on our nerves. But the Bible teaches us to bear with people and forgive them. Take a few minutes and think about the gracious way God has treated you. When you made mistakes, he forgave you. When you weren't acting loveable, God loved you anyway. Write him a letter thanking him for bearing with you and forgiving you.

_____

_____

_____

_____

_____

_____

_____

_____

_____

_____

_____

_____

_____

_____

# WEEKLY REFLECTION

Reflect on all you've learned this week: focusing on kindness, being merciful in relationships, getting through the tough times, and staying positive. Which of these devotions encouraged you the most? Were any particularly challenging? Share in this space why certain devotions really spoke to you. Was it the topic, the way they made you think, or how they made you feel? Don't skimp on details.

# HOW TO MAKE GOD HAPPY

"And without faith it is impossible to please God, because anyone who comes to him must believe that he exists and that he rewards those who earnestly seek him."

-HEBREWS 11:6

The Bible mentions faith a lot. God loves it when his children really trust him. There are so many examples in scripture of people who really walked the walk and lived by faith. Let's make a list of these heroes. Hebrews 11 is a great place to start. Your favorite Bible characters can be another source. Come up with six or seven people and share one way they each expressed or showed faith in him. Write down one way you'd like your faith in God to be greater.

# FEAR OF MISSING OUT

"So do not fear, for I am with you; do not be dismayed, for I am your God. I will strengthen you and help you; I will uphold you with my righteous right hand."

-ISAIAH 41:10

This is one of the most loved verses in the whole Bible. Maybe that's because everyone struggles with fear, doubt, and anxiety. But God tells us not to fear. It seems to be a choice; we can be afraid, or we can choose not to fear. Complete this thought as you read back over the verse: *I can choose not to be afraid by focusing my attention and my thoughts on these things instead . . .*

# THE SECRET TO HAPPINESS

"I am not saying this because I am in need, for I have learned to be content whatever the circumstances. I know what it is to be in need, and I know what it is to have plenty. I have learned the secret of being content in any and every situation, whether well fed or hungry, whether living in plenty or in want."

-PHILIPPIANS 4:11–12

Today's verse encourages us to learn to be content in all circumstances—when we have a little and when we have a lot. This means that in any situation, we can learn to be okay with what we have and who we are. How are you doing within your own life? Are you learning to be content with where you live, your school, your friends, your teachers, your church, and your life?

# STOP GOSSIP IN ITS TRACKS

"A perverse person stirs up conflict, and a gossip separates close friends."
-PROVERBS 16:28

Someone tells someone who tells someone else. It's gossip. Have you ever been hurt by someone else's careless words? I can speak from experience; it never feels good to know that other people are talking about you, especially in a hurtful or negative way. Proverbs reminds us that gossip will separate close friends. So, how can you avoid gossip? How can you be the one who stops the gossip chain? Complete this sentence: *To try to avoid and even stop the gossip, I can . . .*

# GOD'S TO-DO LIST

"Praise the Lord, my soul, and forget not all his benefits—who forgives all your sins and heals all your diseases, who redeems your life from the pit and crowns you with love and compassion, who satisfies your desires with good things so that your youth is renewed like the eagle's."

-PSALM 103:2–5

Are you someone who makes to-do lists? Maybe you keep your plans on your phone or in a calendar. Did you know that God also makes lists? He completes millions of tasks in countless lives every day. What has he done in your life? How has he been gracious and good to you? Write a list of all the things he has done for you in the space below, and then thank God for each one.

# YOUR SPIRITUAL GIFT

"Each of you should use whatever gift you have received to serve others, as faithful stewards of God's grace in its various forms."

-1 PETER 4:10

God created every person with a special gift. Some are especially kind, others are good teachers, and others may be great at organizing things. Take a moment and think about the ways you are gifted and write your answers in the space below.

- What do you love to do to help others?
- How do you like to serve?
- How do you believe God has gifted you?
- In what ways can you use your gifts to serve God and other people?
- How do you believe God specially crafted you to make a difference in this world?

Note: If you have any trouble answering these questions, you might ask a parent, a mentor, or a friend to walk through them with you.

# FILLED TO OVERFLOWING

"May the God of hope fill you with all joy and peace as you trust in him,
so that you may overflow with hope by the power of the Holy Spirit."

-ROMANS 15:13

*Full.* It's such a good word. A full stomach. A full bank account. A fridge full of food. We like things that are full, and so does God. Have you noticed that many prayers in the Bible are for others to be filled up—with joy, peace, and hope? What do you need him to fill today? Is it a longing of your heart? A need that no one knows about? Take a few minutes and ask God to fill your hurting, empty, and needy places.

## WEEKLY REFLECTION

Flip back through the journal entries for this past week. We talked about being content and happy, how God has his own checklist for your life, and what your gifts to the world might be. Look over the things that you wrote. Which prompt caused you to write the most? Why do you suppose this particular devotion captured your attention so much? Take a few moments and share your thoughts here.

# LEARNING FROM OTHERS

"Whatever you have learned or received or heard from me, or seen in me—put it into practice. And the God of peace will be with you."

-PHILIPPIANS 4:9

There is so much in life that we can learn from our friends, family, teachers, pastors, coaches, and even authors of our favorite books or podcasters we love. When you think about those who teach you the most, who are the four or five people that come to mind? Write down their names here. Then go back over your list and share one reason you like learning from each person.

# FEELING LONELY

"Do not fear, for I have redeemed you; I have summoned you by name; you are mine. When you pass through the waters, I will be with you; and when you pass through the rivers, they will not sweep over you. When you walk through the fire, you will not be burned; the flames will not set you ablaze."

-ISAIAH 43:1–2

I remember a time in high school when I felt so alone. I had made the decision to stand up for something that I believed in, and some people didn't respond well. I did the right thing, but it was hard! I felt really lonely and left out. During that time, I was reminded that God is always with me. What does today's verse say about the way God shows he cares for us? For example, he has redeemed us, and called us by name. Use your own words in the space below. Be sure to circle your favorite.

# GOD LOVES MUSIC, TOO

"Praise the Lord. Praise God in his sanctuary; praise him in his mighty heavens. Praise him for his acts of power; praise him for his surpassing greatness. Praise him with the sounding of the trumpet, praise him with the harp and lyre, praise him with timbrel and dancing, praise him with the strings and pipe, praise him with the clash of cymbals, praise him with resounding cymbals."

-PSALM 150:1–5

Worship music is a powerful way to praise God. Some lyrics are taken straight out of the Bible. The words in today's verses were praise songs sung by the Jewish people as they walked to Jerusalem for various festivals. Take a moment and write him a song of praise today. When you're finished, read or sing your song to him.

# FIND REST

"Come to me, all you who are weary and burdened, and I will give you rest. Take my yoke upon you and learn from me, for I am gentle and humble in heart, and you will find rest for your souls. For my yoke is easy and my burden is light."

-MATTHEW 11:28–30

Do you ever find yourself so exhausted you just want to crawl into bed? Maybe you had a tough week of volleyball practice or crammed all night for a test. Jesus invites us to come to him for rest. That's because he offers refreshment for our weary souls. Renewal. Restoration. Replenishment. Recovery. Could you use some real rest? Complete this sentence: *Some of the spaces in my life that need rest are . . .*

# GOD HEARS YOUR PRAYERS

"This is the confidence we have in approaching God: that if
we ask anything according to his will, he hears us."

-1 JOHN 5:14

What great news! God hears our prayers. He's like a loyal BFF who always reads our texts. Knowing that he is really listening, what would you like to say to the Lord today? Write your words to him here. Tell him anything and everything you'd like him to know.

# DON'T CRITICIZE

"Why do you look at the speck of sawdust in your brother's eye and pay no attention to the plank in your own eye? How can you say to your brother, 'Let me take the speck out of your eye,' when all the time there is a plank in your own eye?"

-MATTHEW 7:3–4

It's called "cancel culture." A group of people gets upset with someone and decides to tune them out and ignore them. The Bible tells us not to judge, criticize, or cancel others, though. Our job is to take care of our own issues. God's job is to deal with the issues of others. Complete this sentence: *To behave more like a follower of Christ, I want to treat others . . .*

# YOUR LIFE MOTTO

"The Lord is with me; I will not be afraid. What can mere mortals do to me?
The Lord is with me; he is my helper. I look in triumph on my enemies."

-PSALM 118:6–7

Does your school have a motto that states its beliefs or ideals? What about your favorite athlete or brand? Anyone can adopt a motto to get them through life's challenges. Today's verse contains an encouraging one—"the Lord is with me." Take a few minutes and jot down a few verses, quotes, or sayings that could become one of your life mottos. Choose one to carry around with you today, perhaps inside a notebook, posted in your locker, or pinned to your home screen.

# WEEKLY REFLECTION

This week we talked about what your life motto might be. What are your guiding principles? In your life, you may be standing alone on some issues. Albert Einstein said, "The woman who follows the crowd will usually go no further than the crowd. The woman who walks alone is likely to find herself in places no one has ever been before." How does this encourage you? Share your thoughts below.

# RUN FOR (ETERNAL) LIFE

"Do you not know that in a race all the runners run, but only one gets the prize? Run in such a way as to get the prize. Everyone who competes in the games goes into strict training. They do it to get a crown that will not last, but we do it to get a crown that will last forever. Therefore I do not run like someone running aimlessly . . . "

-1 CORINTHIANS 9:24–26

Let's take a personal assessment today. What do you value most in life? What matters most to you? To really answer this question, write down the following items on the lines below.

- Money
- Fame
- Friends
- Family
- Achievements/Success
- God and my spiritual life
- Other

Now, go back and rank these from 1 to 7. The most important item will be #1, and the least important item will be #7. Look back over your rankings, and ask: Does he fit into your life? Do you need to make adjustments?

.......................................................................................................

.......................................................................................................

.......................................................................................................

.......................................................................................................

.......................................................................................................

.......................................................................................................

.......................................................................................................

# WHAT ARE YOUR WORDS COMMUNICATING?

"Let your conversation be always full of grace, seasoned with
salt, so that you may know how to answer everyone."

-COLOSSIANS 4:6

What sorts of conversations do you have with your friends? What do you love
to talk about? What makes you and your besties laugh so hard you cry? The
Bible tells us to have conversations that are well-seasoned, grace-filled, and wise.
What would that sound like for you? Draw a picture of a mouth or lips. Then,
using a dialogue bubble, write down how you can speak with more grace,
kindness, love, honesty, or wisdom. For example, you might tell your mom how
much you appreciate her—even if she's been stressing you out.

# A TROUBLED WORLD

"I have told you these things, so that in me you may have peace. In this world you will have trouble. But take heart! I have overcome the world."

-JOHN 16:33

Have you ever been to the ocean on a calm day, when the sky is blue, the wind is light, and the water is beautiful? That's the image of peace that I tend to carry in my heart—no matter what's going on around me. Even if trouble surrounds you in the form of girl drama, your parents arguing, crazy world events, or challenging relationships, Jesus gives peace right in the middle of the chaos. What does that peacefulness look like to you?

# DO YOU KNOW THE TRUTH?

"Then you will know the truth, and the truth will set you free."
-JOHN 8:32

Jenny was in 10th grade when a good friend confronted her about her sarcasm. Jenny didn't realize how rude her comments could be. She was simply making jokes! But Jenny soon realized she was also reacting to her parents' divorce. Uncovering this truth set her free. Face a truth you need to hear and let God set you free. Take a moment to journal your thoughts here.

# GOT GRANDPARENTS?

"I am reminded of your sincere faith, which first lived in your grandmother Lois and in your mother Eunice and, I am persuaded, now lives in you also."

-2 TIMOTHY 1:5

What are your grandparents like? How have they influenced your life? Take a few minutes to reflect on their lives. If you don't spend much time with them, ask your parents to tell you some stories. Write down the name of each grandparent in the space below. Beside each name, share one or two things you know about them and one way you may be like them. Are you really tall like your grandfather? Do you have a goofy sense of humor like your grandmother?

# EVERYTHING CHANGES, EXCEPT GOD

"Jesus Christ is the same yesterday and today and forever."
-HEBREWS 13:8

My husband is a person of daily and repetitive routine. It's his way. It keeps him grounded, and it never changes. Did you know that our God is also fond of repetition? He calls the sun to rise every morning. He tells the oceans when to go out and come in every day. And he can be trusted with the cares of your life—every single day. Truly, he is faithful and dependable. Finish this sentence: *Because God never changes, this makes me feel . . .*

# LET'S TALK ABOUT DATING

"Do not be misled: 'Bad company corrupts good character.' "
-1 CORINTHIANS 15:33

Today I'd like you to create a dating checklist. What do you look for in some-one you want to date? What attracts you to another person? I'd like you to create a dating checklist. Come up with 10 to 15 traits you would love to find in another person. Do they love Jesus? Are they kind? Do they make you laugh? Do they treat their parents well? These can apply to everyone you date, because you don't need to date anyone you wouldn't eventually want to marry! Create your checklist below.

## WEEKLY REFLECTION

We covered a myriad of topics this past week. From dating and grandparents, to how everything changes (except God!), to dealing with trouble, to the power of our words. Which topics really had a lasting impact on you? Share a few big ideas that you learned as you completed these devotions. Make a plan to continue learning.

# BE COURAGEOUS

"David also said to Solomon his son, 'Be strong and courageous,
and do the work. Do not be afraid or discouraged, for the LORD God,
my God, is with you. He will not fail you or forsake you until all the
work for the service of the temple of the LORD is finished.' "

-1 CHRONICLES 28:20

Having courage means doing something even if it scares you, feels risky, or makes you nervous. Many years ago, at a high school leadership camp, I had to make an impromptu speech and participate in a debate. There was no time to warm up. I just had to go for it. The Bible encourages us to be strong and bold, to step out in faith, and to trust God. What does courage look like in your life? Maybe you gave a speech in class, climbed a rock wall, confronted a friend, or stood up for something important to you. Describe a time when you had to "go for it."

# TRY TO BE HUMBLE

"When someone invites you to a wedding feast, do not take the place of honor, for a person more distinguished than you may have been invited. If so, the host who invited both of you will come and say to you, 'Give this person your seat' . . . But when you are invited, take the lowest place, so that when your host comes, he will say to you, 'Friend, move up to a better place.' Then you will be honored in the presence of all the other guests. For all those who exalt themselves will be humbled, and those who humble themselves will be exalted."

-LUKE 14:8–11

Do you know someone who is always hogging the spotlight? Maybe you know a guy who brags about his grades or a girl who talks over everyone else. The Bible teaches us to have humility, to let someone else have the spotlight or get the credit—just like Jesus would. This might feel different from what the world around us values. Finish this sentence: *When I think about my own humility, I think . . .*

# GOD, THE FATHER

"The Spirit you received does not make you slaves, so that you live in fear again; rather, the Spirit you received brought about your adoption to sonship. And by him we cry, 'Abba, Father.'"

-ROMANS 8:15

Lindsey was a student of mine whose dad was just not around very much. He left the family when she was a little girl and rarely made time to see her. However, when Lindsey was in fourth grade, someone told her about her heavenly Father and how much he loved her and wanted to adopt her. In time, she learned to talk to God and enjoy the sweetness of a relationship with him. Whether you've had an amazing relationship with your earthly father or a not-so-great one, you can enjoy the love and acceptance of your heavenly Dad. Try writing God a prayer here, explaining how you feel about your relationship with him.

# BROKENNESS IS MESSY

*"The Lord is close to the brokenhearted and saves those who are crushed in spirit."*
-PSALM 34:18

I had just pulled a glass bowl from my cabinet when my hands slipped, and the bowl crashed onto our granite countertop. It shattered into hundreds of pieces—what a mess! We spent over an hour getting the little glass fragments out of the carpet. Heartache can make you feel shattered like that. Have you ever had a bad breakup, been ghosted by a friend, gotten a bad grade when you worked hard, or been criticized by a coach? God says that he is close to those whose hearts are broken. Finish this thought: *Because God is near when my heart is broken . . .*

# GOD SINGS OVER YOU

"The Lord your God is with you, the Mighty Warrior who saves.
He will take great delight in you; in his love he will no longer
rebuke you, but will rejoice over you with singing."

-ZEPHANIAH 3:17

Here's a fun secret: I've always wanted to be a soloist. You know, the girl who gets asked to sing the big numbers at church and carry the lead roles. Unfortunately, I'm just not the soloist type, though it still makes my heart happy to carry a tune. Whether you're a vocal diva or not, singing can express delight and happiness. The Bible tells us that God loves to sing—to us. What do you imagine his voice is like? What songs might he sing to us?

# MEDICINE FOR THE HEART

"A cheerful heart is good medicine, but a crushed spirit dries up the bones."
-PROVERBS 17:22

Your emotions affect your health. According to the Integrative Medicine Center of Western Colorado, studies have shown that having joy and being cheerful acts like good medication. Laughing can boost your immune system and help you live a long life. On the other hand, sadness and despair can wreak havoc on your health. Chronic sadness can even weaken your bones. How do your emotions impact your body? Are you drying up your bones or improving your immune system? Detail your thoughts here.

# WHAT'S HEAVEN LIKE?

"He will wipe every tear from their eyes. There will be no more death or mourning or crying or pain, for the old order of things has passed away."

-REVELATION 21:4

I want you to think about heaven for a bit. The Bible tells us there will be no sadness, crying, pain, or death in heaven. Can you imagine what that might look and feel like? Draw a picture of what you envision heaven to be. Add some words to your picture to describe the scene.

## WEEKLY REFLECTION

This week we thought a lot about God—who he is, how he sings over us, and what heaven might be like. Take a few minutes to review the prompts and then consider who God is to you. In your opinion, what is God really like? If he were a really close friend, how would you describe him to your friends and family? Share your thoughts in the space below.

# DON'T BE DERAILED

*"I can do all this through him who gives me strength."*
-PHILIPPIANS 4:13

A few weeks ago, my neighbor Megan, a senior in high school, shared some of her dreams for the future. She is excited about what's to come, but she really struggles with anxiety. Megan has big plans, but she often lets her fears and insecurities hold her back. I'll ask you the same questions I asked her. What would you do if you weren't afraid? What would you attempt? Write about it here. (And then I dare you to do it!)

# GOD WILL FIGHT FOR YOU!

"... Do not be afraid. Stand firm and you will see the deliverance the Lord will bring you today ... The Lord will fight for you; you need only to be still."

-EXODUS 14:13–14

When I was 12 years old, a bully in my neighborhood wanted to hurt me. Luckily, an older neighbor boy stood in between us, and I wasn't harmed in any way. God promises to fight for us like that. What does that look like to you? Maybe he will calm someone down or prompt them to leave you alone. Maybe he will divert their attention or move you out of a bad situation. Finish this thought: *Because the Bible promises that God will fight for me, I ...*

# SPECIAL MOMENTS

"Joshua set up the twelve stones that had been in the middle of
the Jordan at the spot where the priests who carried the ark of
the covenant had stood. And they are there to this day."

-JOSHUA 4:9

What moments have made you feel special? For me, I think of the time I was
invited to be part of the freshman leadership team at my college. One girl and
one guy were chosen to represent our class, and some older students picked me.
It made me feel so special! Write about a time in your life that lifted you up.

# PRACTICE PATIENCE

"Be completely humble and gentle; be patient, bearing with one another in love."
-EPHESIANS 4:2

When I drive, I sometimes get really impatient with traffic, long red lights, or other drivers. Do you ever have trouble staying patient? When your best friend is late again, how do you respond? When the lesson in class is boring, do you get restless? When the coach gives the other girls more playing time than you, how do you handle it? The Bible encourages us to be gentle and patient, and to bear with others. How might you become a more patient and compassionate person? Make a list of four to five action steps you might take to become more patient with others.

# YOU CAN BE SAVED

"For it is with your heart that you believe and are justified, and it is with your mouth that you profess your faith and are saved. As Scripture says, 'Anyone who believes in him will never be put to shame.' For there is no difference between Jew and Gentile—the same LORD is LORD of all and richly blesses all who call on him, for, 'Everyone who calls on the name of the LORD will be saved.'"

-ROMANS 10:10–13

Salvation is a sweet gift that God offers to every single person on this earth. I received my gift when I was in the sixth grade. Have you received the gift of salvation? If so, share the details of your experience here. If not, why not invite Jesus into your life today? It's easy—just give all you know of you to all you know of him. Invite him to be your Savior and start your relationship today. Write out your prayer to God in the lines below.

## NOTHING CAN SEPARATE YOU FROM GOD

"No, in all these things we are more than conquerors through him
who loved us. For I am convinced that neither death nor life, neither
angels nor demons, neither the present nor the future, nor any powers,
neither height nor depth, nor anything else in all creation, will be able to
separate us from the love of God that is in Christ Jesus our Lord."

-ROMANS 8:37–39

I once got separated from my friends in an airport in a foreign country. It was
really scary until I found them again. In contrast, the Bible tells us that nothing
can ever separate us from God and his love. Nothing! There is no person, sin,
hurt, or difficulty that can come between us and the Father. We can't get away
from him. We can't get lost. Finish this sentence: *I'm so glad that nothing can
separate me from God because . . .*

# TWO ARE BETTER THAN ONE

"Two are better than one, because they have a good return for
their labor: If either of them falls down, one can help the other up.
But pity anyone who falls and has no one to help them up."

-ECCLESIASTES 4:9–10

Friends who stick with us are the best: those who walk in when everyone else is walking out, who stand by you when you are going through a rough patch, and who listen when you share your heart. These are your real BFFs. Write the names of some of your true friends in the space here. Then, explain what you appreciate about each friend. If you get the chance today, tell them how grateful you are for their friendship.

## WEEKLY REFLECTION

We read many wonderful promises of truth about you and God over the past seven days. I've listed several of these here. Choose the one that you appreciate the most. Write about why you love it. Then, take a moment to pray and thank God for this promise.

✗ Nothing can separate you from God's love. Nothing!

✗ God can save you and anyone else who believes in him.

✗ God will fight for you! You don't need to be afraid.

✗ God can give you strength to accomplish all things.

# GETTING BAD NEWS

"They will have no fear of bad news; their hearts are steadfast, trusting in the Lord."
-PSALM 112:7

As you've probably figured out, life isn't always kittens and rainbows. Maybe one of your friends is moving away with their family. Perhaps you know someone who is feeling depressed. Maybe a friend or family member has cancer. Whatever the case, bad news stinks. But the Bible tells us that we don't have to be afraid of it. Our hearts can remain steadfast and calm—no matter what we hear—because we can talk everything over with the Lord. In this space, "talk out" the issues with God that are weighing on your heart.

# BE BOLD ABOUT YOUR FAITH

"But in your hearts revere Christ as Lord. Always be prepared to give an answer to everyone who asks you to give the reason for the hope that you have. But do this with gentleness and respect . . ."

-1 PETER 3:15

Honesty time . . . have you ever felt really uncomfortable when someone asked you about your faith? Have you wanted to hide when you were put on the spot about God? Sometimes it's hard to be bold about our faith. But the Bible encourages us to be ready to respectfully tell people about Jesus. What are some practical ways you can become more comfortable—and confident—in sharing your faith? Write your ideas here.

# HOW TO BE BLESSED

"Blessed is the one who does not walk in step with the wicked or stand in the way that sinners take or sit in the company of mockers, but whose delight is in the law of the Lord, and who meditates on his law day and night. That person is like a tree planted by streams of water, which yields its fruit in season and whose leaf does not wither—whatever they do prospers."

-PSALM 1:1–3

My daughter's friend Hannah had a tough choice. Two groups of friends at school were vying for her attention. One group was made up of beautiful, popular people, but they were ungodly and tended to pursue the wrong things. The other group wasn't as appealing on the outside but was filled with friends who sought to live in a God-honoring way. If Hannah came to you and asked you how she could choose between these groups, what would you tell her? Share your advice here.

## AS WISE AS YOUR TEACHERS

"I have more insight than all my teachers, for I meditate on your statutes."
-PSALM 119:99

Who are your favorite teachers? What's awesome about them? Are they funny or wise? Do they tell great stories? How have they encouraged you? Take a minute and journal about how you appreciate these teachers. Then, if you are feeling really brave, I'd like you to text them, email them, or write them a nice note. (I was a teacher, and I saved every nice note I ever received from a student!)

# WALKING WITH INTEGRITY

"Whoever walks in integrity walks securely, but whoever takes crooked paths will be found out."

-PROVERBS 10:9

Writer Jim Stovall once said, "Integrity is doing the right thing, even if nobody is watching." Integrity leads you to go the extra mile: pay back the friend to whom you owe money, be honest and tell your parents where you're going, and eat a healthy dinner, even if your parents are out for the night. Integrity isn't always easy; in fact, it's a lot of extra work. But if you live with integrity, you will sleep better at night. It lets you walk securely and in peace. Describe an event or a situation when you did what was right. How did this choice make you feel?

## NAVIGATING STRONG EMOTIONS

"Better a patient person than a warrior, one with
self-control than one who takes a city."

-PROVERBS 16:32

My friend Kendall is a person of great self-control. She takes time to consider
her answers and responds calmly (most of the time) to the chaos around her.
My friend Taylor, however, tends to blow up. She has little patience and reacts
quickly to everything. Her hair-trigger temper has hurt many people around
her, and she often has to apologize. When you think about your own emotions,
which of my friends do you most relate to and why?

# FORGIVENESS

"Then Peter came to Jesus and asked, 'Lord, how many times shall I forgive my brother or sister who sins against me? Up to seven times?' Jesus answered, 'I tell you, not seven times, but seventy-seven times.'"

-MATTHEW 18:21–22

Do you have a person in your life who you have to forgive over and over again? I don't have to forgive my friend, Terri, for the careless things she tends to say. The Bible tells us to let offenses go each time we are wronged, even if the other person never apologizes. Talk about difficult! How can we do that? Make a list of seven ways you can begin to really let go of your anger and hurt. For example, pray for the person who hurt you, and ask God to heal what is broken in their life. With empathy, try to see things from their point of view.

# WEEKLY REFLECTION

Look back over your notes from the past week. We talked about fighting anger, hurt, and disappointment, and being confident in your faith. Which of these was your favorite? What did you love about it? What is God teaching you? How will you continue your work? Write down your thoughts in the space provided.

# THAT'S WHY IT'S CALLED GRACE

"And if by grace, then it cannot be based on works; if
it were, grace would no longer be grace."

-ROMANS 11:6

Grace. It may be my favorite word in the entire Bible. Songs have been written about it. People love to talk about it. But what is grace, really? Put simply, it's being kind to someone no matter how they treat you. God has shown us grace and wants us to show grace to others. Who might need a little more grace from you today? Finish this sentence: *If I were to show grace to everyone today . . .*

# GROWING INTO AN ADULT

"Don't let anyone look down on you because you are young, but set an example for the believers in speech, in conduct, in love, in faith, and in purity."

-1 TIMOTHY 4:12

Just for fun, I want you to draw two pictures of yourself on this page. First, draw a picture or a cartoon of your current self, and then draw yourself at age 25. Write down a few words next to the picture of your current self that describe you right now. Then, beside the picture of your future self, write down a few words to describe who you will become.

# HELPING OTHERS

"Give, and it will be given to you. A good measure, pressed down, shaken together and running over, will be poured into your lap. For with the measure you use, it will be measured to you."

-LUKE 6:38

As a teenaged girl, you have much to offer the world: your insights, your unique perspective, your talents, your passions, your gifts, and your sense of humor. The Bible encourages us to give , so how can you use these God-given traits to help others? In fact, we are told that if we give, we will receive great blessings. In the space below, list 10 ways you can help or serve others this week. Start by doing at least one of them today.

# TAKE EVERY THOUGHT CAPTIVE

"We demolish arguments and every pretension that sets itself up against the knowledge of God, and we take captive every thought to make it obedient to Christ."

-2 CORINTHIANS 10:5

Have you ever experienced fighting a lot of mosquitos or gnats when you were outside? It's annoying, right? Sometimes the thoughts flying around in our head are just as pesky. That's why the Bible tells us that we have to catch our thoughts and get control of them. How can you do this? Maybe listen to Christian podcasts or music, read the Bible, or talk to a trusted friend. Write down three to four practical ways you can take every thought captive.

# BEST USE OF TIME

*" 'I have the right to do anything,' you say—but not everything is beneficial. 'I have the right to do anything'—but not everything is constructive."*

-1 CORINTHIANS 10:23

My health coach, Doug, challenged me recently on how I spend my time. I, like most people, watch too much TV and spend too much time on my devices. Doug suggested I spend more time reading, exercising, praying, and talking with people I care about. But, to do this, I have to give up some TV and screen time. If you wanted to spend more time reading, exercising, praying, or hanging out with friends and family, what would you need to give up? Name three or four things here. For an extra stretch, make a goal for the next week.

# STEP INTO THE NEW

"Forget the former things; do not dwell on the past. See, I am doing a new thing! Now it springs up; do you not perceive it? I am making a way in the wilderness and streams in the wasteland."

-ISAIAH 43:18–19

What's the last new thing you bought for yourself or got as a gift: shoes, a song to stream, new jeans? We all love new things. Think about it for a moment. What new thing has God done in your life recently? Maybe he sent you a new friend or a teacher you really like. Possibly, he opened a door for you to be on a team. Maybe he gave you a new ministry or mission. Complete this sentence: *I'm so grateful that God has given me this new . . .*

# WAIT ON GOD

"I remain confident of this: I will see the goodness of the Lord in the land of the living. Wait for the Lord; be strong and take heart and wait for the Lord."

-PSALM 27:13–14

Emma, a ninth grader in my church, hates to wait. Since she can't drive, she has to wait for rides all the time. And she hates to wait on her brothers and sisters. Most of all, she despises having to wait for God to answer her prayers—especially one she has been praying about for years: She wants her parents to reunite. If Emma shared her wish with you, what are three or four ways you might encourage her to more patiently wait on God? Share your advice here.

# WEEKLY REFLECTION

As you journaled and studied this past week, you spent a good deal of time thinking about growing up, changing, and becoming more mature. In thinking about your life, how are you growing and changing? What are you most pleased about? What are you still working on and hoping will get better? Share some of your thoughts about your personal growth here. (For example, how do you feel about your spiritual, mental, or physical growth?)

# FITTING IN

"Am I now trying to win the approval of human beings, or of God? Or am I trying to please people? If I were still trying to please people, I would not be a servant of Christ."

-GALATIANS 1:10

Approval is a big deal to most girls. We want to fit in, look gorgeous, get more likes, be included, and feel like we matter. Even grown women feel this way! But the Bible tells us we have a choice. We can either spend our lives seeking the approval of others or seeking the approval of God. How can you work on seeking God's approval more than other people's? Finish this thought: *If I stopped trying to be a people-pleaser and instead tried to be a God-pleaser, then . . .*

........................................................................

........................................................................

........................................................................

........................................................................

........................................................................

........................................................................

........................................................................

........................................................................

........................................................................

........................................................................

........................................................................

........................................................................

........................................................................

# FAITHFUL FRIENDS

"Whoever can be trusted with very little can also be trusted with much, and whoever is dishonest with very little will also be dishonest with much."

-LUKE 16:10

Stephanie is a reliable friend. She shows up when she says she will. She does what she says she is going to do. I find myself trusting her almost more than anyone else I know. Who fills this role in your life? What do they look like, how do they act, what do they do and not do? Draw a picture of your most faithful friend. Then, beside the picture, write a few traits describing this friend. Finally, explain why you chose this person.

# LOVE WHEN YOU'RE READY

*"Daughters of Jerusalem, I charge you: Do not arouse
or awaken love until it so desires."*

-SONG OF SOLOMON 8:4

Being a teenage girl today is a special privilege. In today's world, you get to set the boundaries for your life. You get to choose whose hand you will hold, who will kiss you and who won't, and who and what will get close to you and your body. God has given you the privilege of opening the door of intimacy only when you are ready. Write out a prayer about how this makes you feel. Talk this over with God. (You may want to talk this over with a parent or a trusted mentor as well.)

# WORTH MORE THAN GOLD

"How much better to get wisdom than gold, to get insight rather than silver!"
-PROVERBS 16:16

To be wise is to be well-informed, perceptive, and insightful. Wisdom, according to Pastor Adrian Rogers, is "seeing life from God's point of view." How do we do this? How do we become wiser? For me, I hung out with older students who seemed to have it together. I went to Bible study and joined a mentoring group. Youth group was helpful for me, too. What about you? In the space here, list seven to eight ways you can gain more wisdom and insight. For example, you might hang out with wise people, read great books, listen to podcasts, and pray for wisdom.

# OVERCOME STRESS

"I keep my eyes always on the Lord. With him at my right
hand, I will not be shaken. Therefore my heart is glad and
my tongue rejoices; my body also will rest secure."

-PSALM 16:8–9

Megan was stressed. She had volleyball practice, two exams, a family event, and
youth group—all happening on the same day, and nearly the same time! Does
this sound like your life? Many teen girls feel overwhelmed with everything
they have to do. Maybe you are dealing with that stress, too. Write down your
six or seven biggest stressors—those things that put the most pressure on you.
Then, pray over each one. Remember, with God's help, we will not be shaken!

# MAKE ADJUSTMENTS

"Do not lie to each other, since you have taken off the old self with its practices and have put on the new self, which is being renewed in the knowledge of its Creator."

-COLOSSIANS 3:9–10

New shoes are often a little uncomfortable at first. They have to be worn in a bit before they really fit right. Likewise, the Christian life needs regular adjustment. Sometimes it's a little uncomfortable as we learn new principles and grow in our faith. It's also hard to change old behaviors and habits. Read the questions below and answer them in the space provided.

x What adjustments has God been making in your life?
x What has he been teaching you?
x How has God been stretching your faith?

# LOVE YOUR NEIGHBORS

"'The most important one,' answered Jesus, 'is this: . . . Love the Lord your God with all your heart and with all your soul and with all your mind and with all your strength. The second is this: Love your neighbor as yourself. There is no commandment greater than these.'"

-MARK 12:29–31

My family friend, Ashley, is such an awesome friend to others. Several times a week she sends texts to her friends just because. She also loves to give gifts when friends are going through a hard time. Her gifts often come with a sweet and encouraging note. How are you doing to love, support, and encourage those in your world? List four to five practical ways you can love the people you know.

Friendships and relationships were important topics we covered this week. One of my favorite friendship quotes comes from C. S. Lewis, author of the famous *Chronicles of Narnia* series: "Friendship is born at that moment when one person says to another, 'What! You too? I thought I was the only one.'" What do you think about this idea? Do you agree? Use the space here to describe two or three friends who like the same things you do.

# GROWING IN WISDOM

*"And Jesus grew in wisdom and stature, and in favor with God and man."*
-LUKE 2:52

Growth spurts happen fairly often in a teenager's life. Perhaps you've even had one this year. In what other ways are you growing as a person? In the space here, consider some of the ways that you are stretching, learning, and changing. Write about these things:

- ✕ I'm growing up physically in these ways.
- ✕ I'm growing emotionally in these ways.
- ✕ I'm growing in my relationships in these ways.
- ✕ I'm growing closer to God in these ways.
- ✕ I'm growing financially in these ways.

# MAKING THE BEST DECISIONS

"Trust in the LORD with all your heart and lean not on your own understanding; in all your ways submit to him, and he will make your paths straight."

-PROVERBS 3:5–6

As you move through life, you'll make some very important decisions. For example, my niece Emily is deciding where to go to college. She's talked to her parents, friends, teachers, coaches, and guidance counselor, but she still isn't sure what to do. If she came to you, what would you tell her? Using today's verses and your own life experiences, write out your best advice to Emily here.

# COMPARISON IS THE THIEF OF ALL JOY

"We do not dare to classify or compare ourselves with some who commend themselves. When they measure themselves by themselves and compare themselves with themselves, they are not wise."

-2 CORINTHIANS 10:12

Do you ever compare yourself to other girls? Women? Celebrities? The Kardashians? It's so easy—especially as girls—to look at what others are doing, wearing, or accomplishing, or who they're dating. The Bible tells us it's not wise or beneficial to measure ourselves by those standards. What if we learn, instead, to celebrate who God made us to be? In the space provided below, have a mini-celebration of who God uniquely crafted you to be. Write down 10 reasons that you are a one-of-a-kind original, a girl beyond comparison (you know, those cute freckles, that great smile, your kind heart, your jump shot). Thank God for the way he made you.

# DOING YOUR BEST

"Whatever you do, work at it with all your heart, as working for the Lord, not for human masters, since you know that you will receive an inheritance from the Lord as a reward. It is the Lord Christ you are serving."

-COLOSSIANS 3:23–24

Sometimes we are afraid to try new things because we think we might fail. An opportunity might arise, but we don't want to blow it, so we don't step out with courage. We should push ourselves to do things anyway, even if we are afraid. There are so many amazing adventures out there for you, but they may be on the other side of your fear. Let me ask you some honest questions today: What are you avoiding? What would you love to do but are scared to try? What is holding you back? How awesome might it be if you went for it anyway?

# WALKING THROUGH DARKNESS

"Even though I walk through the darkest valley, I will fear no evil, for you are with me; your rod and your staff, they comfort me."

-PSALM 23:4

A teenager from my church, Savannah, just walked through a dark valley with her family. Savannah's mother had passed away from cancer. Her family is struggling with the loss. Maybe you can relate? Possibly you've lost a loved one, dealt with cancer, or suffered some other significant loss in your life. How have you found God's comfort in the valleys? Write about your experiences here.

# EXPECT MORE

"Now to him who is able to do immeasurably more than all we ask or imagine, according to his power that is at work within us, to him be glory in the church and in Christ Jesus throughout all generations, for ever and ever! Amen."

-EPHESIANS 3:20–21

God can do immeasurably more than all we might ask or think. What do you want God to do for you or with you in your life right now? Write down some of these desires here. Pray and invite God to do amazing things in your life. Be specific. Tell him what you'd love to see in your family, friend group, church, community, on your team, in your mission, in your calling, in your future, and in your life.

# FRIENDS IN FAITH

"Do not be yoked together with unbelievers. For what do righteousness and wickedness have in common? Or what fellowship can light have with darkness?"

-2 CORINTHIANS 6:14

Maria has the most amazing friends. They pray for her, push her toward better things, and inspire her to be the best version of herself. What about your friends? Do they support you, motivate you, make you better? In the space provided, write down the names of your three best friends. Then, note how each one encourages you and inspires you. (If you don't have three great friends, write about those you do have, then pray and invite God to give you more of these.)

This week we talked a lot about growing—stretching your faith, getting wiser, making better decisions, and becoming brave. Take a moment and look over the titles; feel free to go back over your notes if needed. In the space below, share why you particularly connected with one or any number of these topics.

# ALL THINGS FOR GOOD

"You intended to harm me, but God intended it for good to accomplish what is now being done, the saving of many lives."

-GENESIS 50:20

We hear this phrase often: God works all things for good. Do you believe this? Have you found it to be true in your own life? If so, describe the situation here. If not, pray and invite God to bring good out of any hurtful and challenging circumstances. You can pray about your parents' divorce, your accident, not making the team, or not being asked out by the person you like.

# TAKE THE HIGH ROAD

"For we are taking pains to do what is right, not only in the eyes of the Lord but also in the eyes of man."

-2 CORINTHIANS 8:21

Taking the high road means doing what's right no matter what everyone else is doing. It's being kind to the girl no one likes at school. It's babysitting your little sister when you'd rather not. In this space, talk about a time when you took the high road. How did it make you feel? Do you think anyone noticed? How do you think God felt about your decision to do the right thing?

# FRIENDS ARE PATIENT, FRIENDS ARE KIND

> "Love is patient, love is kind. It does not envy, it does not boast, it is not proud. It does not dishonor others, it is not self-seeking, it is not easily angered, and it keeps no record of wrongs. Love does not delight in evil but rejoices with the truth. It always protects, always trusts, always hopes, and always perseveres. Love never fails."

-1 CORINTHIANS 13:4–8A

Checklists are quick ways for us to consider a lot of information quickly. The verses above read like a checklist for a great friend. Look over the items and write down the name of one friend beside each. Once you have gone through the entire list, write out a prayer thanking God for each of your amazing friends.

✕ *My patient friend is* . . .

✕ *My kind friend is* . . .

✕ *My humble friend is* . . .

✕ *My friend who honors others is* . . .

✕ *My friend who doesn't anger easily is* . . .

✕ *My friend who rejoices in truth is* . . .

✕ *My friend who protects is* . . .

✕ *My friend who trusts others is* . . .

✕ *My friend who always hopes is* . . .

# IT CAN BE HARD TO OBEY YOUR PARENTS

"Children, obey your parents in the Lord, for this is right. 'Honor your father and mother'—which is the first commandment with a promise—'so that it may go well with you and that you may enjoy long life on the earth.'"

-EPHESIANS 6:1–3

When I was in eighth grade, a bunch of my friends were going to see a movie that my parents didn't want me to see. I went anyway. I decided I was old enough to see this movie. Ironically, I didn't enjoy the experience. I felt horrible the entire time because I knew how much it would hurt them. The Bible tells us that life will be better for us when we honor and obey our parents. It's always a choice! Complete this sentence: *When I disobey my parents, I feel . . .*

## ONE BODY, MANY PARTS

"For just as each of us has one body with many members, and these members do not all have the same function, so in Christ we, though many, form one body, and each member belongs to all the others. We have different gifts, according to the grace given to each of us."

-ROMANS 12:4–6A

Recently, I spoke at an event that featured a praise band. The band was made up of a keyboard player, a guitar player, and a cajón (the box you sit on to play as a drum) player. I was amazed at how their different talents and personalities blended together to craft awesome music. It's like that in life, too. We all have something to add. In thinking about your own life, what do you feel that you contribute to the world? Describe some of your God-given gifts and abilities that make the "song of life" sweeter for those around you.

# FORGIVENESS, ALWAYS

"If we confess our sins, he is faithful and just and will forgive us our sins and purify us from all unrighteousness."

-1 JOHN 1:9

Have you ever done something you really regret? Said the wrong thing at the wrong time? Hurt someone's feelings? Tried something harmful that you shouldn't have? All God's children have blown it at one time or another. I know I have! But here's the beautiful truth about our awesome God: He is faithful to forgive. We can't out-sin God's grace. There is nothing we can do to make him stop loving us. So if there is something you need to make right, talk to God about it today. Write out a prayer here and thank him for his forgiveness and his grace.

# THE GOLDEN RULE

"Do to others as you would have them do to you."
-LUKE 6:31

Have you noticed that some of the best things you learned were taught to you in kindergarten? It's likely that you learned today's verse as a young child. Most of us were taught to treat others the way that we want to be treated. What if we take it even further? Read over the following questions and write down your thoughts below.

✗ What if we give to others, expecting nothing in return?
✗ What might that look like?
✗ How might that make you feel?
✗ How do you think God might bless your kindness?

# WEEKLY REFLECTION

Take a few moments and look back through your notes and the devotionals for the past week. Some of these topics may have been a little convicting or stepped on your toes. Which of the devotions really caused you to stop and think? Which one had you wanting to make some changes? How are you better because of what you read and wrote this week? Share your thoughts here.

# DO NOT BE AFRAID

"The Lord is my light and my salvation—whom shall I fear? The Lord is the stronghold of my life—of whom shall I be afraid?"

-PSALM 27:1

One of my best friends is a fearful person. I call her a champion worrier. She dreams up things that might happen or are within the realm of possibility. Maybe you can relate? We serve a powerful God upon whom we can depend. I've listed five ways you begin to win over fear. Choose two or three of these options and write about how you think these may help you.

1. Start a prayer journal and write out your concerns and prayers to the Lord each day.
2. Ask a mentor or encouraging family member to pray with you to have greater courage.
3. Write out and memorize Psalm 27:1.
4. Admit to a close friend that you struggle with anxiety. Talk about how to overcome and win over fear.

# GOD LOVES EVERY FRECKLE

"Indeed, the very hairs of your head are all numbered. Don't
be afraid; you are worth more than many sparrows."

-LUKE 12:7

God knows everything there is to know about you. He is intricately involved in
the details of your life. From the number of hairs on your head to the color of
your nail polish to the deepest concern of your heart, God knows. How does
this make you feel? Complete this thought: *Because God knows every detail about
me and my life, I can trust him to . . .*

--------------------------------------------------------

--------------------------------------------------------

--------------------------------------------------------

--------------------------------------------------------

--------------------------------------------------------

--------------------------------------------------------

--------------------------------------------------------

--------------------------------------------------------

--------------------------------------------------------

--------------------------------------------------------

--------------------------------------------------------

--------------------------------------------------------

--------------------------------------------------------

# THE SWEETNESS OF CONFESSION

"For as high as the heavens are above the earth, so great is his
love for those who fear him; as far as the east is from the west,
so far has he removed our transgressions from us."

-PSALM 103:11–12

My friend Amy called me one afternoon, so upset. She had made a terrible
mistake that haunted her and kept her up at night. She felt so guilty and sad. I
encouraged her with today's verses and the promise that God always forgives.
Because of his great love, we can run to him with our mistakes, confident that
he can make things right again. Think about a time when you made a mistake
and how it stayed with you. How do these verses encourage you?

# STAND UNITED

"I appeal to you, brothers and sisters, in the name of our Lord Jesus Christ, that all of you agree with one another in what you say and that there be no divisions among you, but that you be perfectly united in mind and thought."

-1 CORINTHIANS 1:10

When I was a senior in high school, I played on the most amazing basketball team. Since we had been a team for years under the same coach, we worked really well together—and we won a lot of games! Have you ever been part of a team, group, or club that worked that well? What was it like? What did you enjoy most? Share your experience.

# UNCOVER THINGS TO GOD

"There is nothing concealed that will not be disclosed, or hidden that will not be made known. What you have said in the dark will be heard in the daylight, and what you have whispered in the ear in the inner rooms will be proclaimed from the roofs."

-LUKE 12:2–3

As a teen, I started journaling. My parents bought me notebooks, and I would write out my prayers, thoughts, struggles, and ideas. To this day, I still write in a journal. There is something so healing and freeing about writing out your thoughts—good and bad—with a pen on paper. Take a few minutes and write about whatever you're thinking now in the space here. You can make your words a prayer (God already knows about it anyway!) or just write down ideas below.

# SEE MORE CLEARLY

"Therefore, I urge you, brothers and sisters, in view of God's mercy, to offer your bodies as a living sacrifice, holy and pleasing to God—this is your true and proper worship. Do not conform to the pattern of this world, but be transformed by the renewing of your mind. Then you will be able to test and approve what God's will is—his good, pleasing, and perfect will."

-ROMANS 12:1–2

Often, I pray for clarity—the ability to really see and understand the issues in my life. I want to be perceptive and wise, so I ask God to renew my mind and give me insight. What are you struggling with right now? Friendship drama? An annoying sibling? A hard class? Write about your struggles here. Invite God to give you clarity and insight into how to handle each one.

# WHO ARE YOUR PEOPLE?

"And let us consider how we may spur one another on toward love and good deeds, not giving up meeting together, as some are in the habit of doing, but encouraging one another—and all the more as you see the Day approaching."

-HEBREWS 10:24–25

If I were to visit your school, where would I find you? Would you be hanging out with kids in the library or the kids who play sports, or the kids who act in plays? Do you like to be with just one person, or are you the girl with many friends? Maybe you are homeschooled and only see your friends at youth group or meetings. Whatever the case, the people you hang out with are "your people." So, tell me about them. What do they like, talk about, look like, etc.?

## WEEKLY REFLECTION

This week we talked about how much God loves you and knows you. As Pastor Tony Campolo says, "God carries your picture in his wallet." You are near and dear to God's heart. He loves you, and your life greatly matters to him. As you reflect over the past week, how have you been reminded of God's love for you?

# FIND CONTENTMENT

"Keep your lives free from the love of money and be content with what you have, because God has said, 'Never will I leave you; never will I forsake you.' "

-HEBREWS 13:5

Do you ever want more than you have right now? More money, clothes, friends, attention from boys (or girls)? The Bible tells us to be content with what we have. But this can sometimes be challenging for us—especially as girls! Today make a list of everything you are really grateful for. You might include your clothes, jewelry, shoes, makeup, books, furniture, car, your great mind, awards, your sense of humor, health, home, family, or friends. Write out some things that you already have, and thank God for them.

# GIVE GENEROUSLY

"Remember this: Whoever sows sparingly will also reap sparingly, and whoever sows generously will also reap generously. Each of you should give what you have decided in your heart to give, not reluctantly or under compulsion, for God loves a cheerful giver. And God is able to bless you abundantly, so that in all things at all times, having all that you need, you will abound in every good work."

-2 CORINTHIANS 9:6–8

I'm not much of a gardener, but there are a few things I've been able to grow from seeds: cucumbers, lima beans, and lots and lots of mint. In life, we also have to plant seeds—seeds of friendship, hard work, generosity, and kindness. What are you planting? Where are you investing your time, money, and energy? Friends? Job? Schoolwork? List three or four of these.

# COMPREHENDING GOD'S LOVE

". . . And I pray that you, being rooted and established in love, may have power, together with all the Lord's holy people, to grasp how wide and long and high and deep is the love of Christ, and to know this love that surpasses knowledge—that you may be filled to the measure of all the fullness of God."

-EPHESIANS 3:17–19

There are concepts in life that are really hard to really grasp. Some are silly—like why we can't get the toothpaste back into the tube. Some are more profound—like how to understand gravity, infinity, or love. God's love is beyond our comprehension, but it's something that we should pray to understand better. He loves you. Period. And he wants you to really grasp this and let it change you. Write out a prayer here, inviting God to show you how much he adores you.

# SECURE IN YOURSELF

"Therefore I tell you, do not worry about your life, what you
will eat or drink; or about your body, what you will wear. Is not
life more than food, and the body more than clothes?"

-MATTHEW 6:25

My friend Brooke is beautiful and talented, but so insecure. Most people would
never know it, but she really struggles with self-doubt. Over the years, I've
watched her hold herself back and live safely because she didn't think she was
good enough. She's missed out on so much because of this. Do you also struggle
with insecurity and self-doubt? How have you let your worries hold you back?
What might happen if you give your worries to God and step out in faith—no
matter how you feel? What might happen if you do things scared, but still do
them? Write about this here.

# KINDNESS IS ALWAYS IN STYLE

"Finally, all of you, be like-minded, be sympathetic, love
one another, be compassionate and humble."

-1 PETER 3:8

What is your style? Are you into colors or muted tones? Do you wear the latest trends, or are you more classic? You may still be figuring that out. Whatever the case, the Bible encourages us to be kind, loving, compassionate, and humble. These things are always in style. List four to five ways you can add more kindness and compassion to your day. To whom can you reach out? How can you give grace? How can you be a better friend?

# MIRACLES STILL HAPPEN

"I am the Lord, the God of all mankind. Is anything too hard for me?"
-JEREMIAH 32:27

Recently, one of my prayer partners issued a challenge to our group. She asked us if we really trusted God enough to pray BIG prayers. Did we believe God could do anything, any time, for any person? I had to answer with a sad NO. Later on, I thought about my friend's questions. I asked God for the courage to pray big prayers and to believe that nothing is too hard for him. Then I made a list of 16 big prayer requests that I'd love to see God answer. In the space here, write down four or five (or 16!) big prayer requests. Talk these over with God and invite him to do bigger things in your life.

# PROTECT YOURSELF ONLINE

"Turn my eyes away from worthless things;
preserve my life according to your word."

-PSALM 119:37

It's fair to say that many of us spend a lot of our time online—especially teens! Most of us use the internet in multiple ways each day. Although it's an amazing tool, we have to be careful. There is so much junk to watch out for: graphic violence, predators, pornography, and more. As you think about the time you spend online, what are some ways you can protect yourself from unsafe sites, dangerous people, and unwanted drama? Make a list of three to four protections you can put in place to keep yourself safe.

Here are some examples:

✗ Set strong passwords.
✗ Turn off your phone at night.
✗ Don't DM anyone you don't really know—especially guys.
✗ Get an app that tells you how much time you spend online each day.

# WEEKLY REFLECTION

Over the course of the past week, we talked about protecting yourself online, believing in BIG miracles, and being grateful for your stuff. What was your greatest lesson of the week? Which one caused you to write the most? Share your thoughts here.

## ALL THINGS WORK TOGETHER FOR GOD

"And we know that in all things God works for the good of those who love him, who have been called according to his purpose."

-ROMANS 8:28

"It will all work out" or "everything will be okay." We hear these phrases all the time, especially when we're faced with a stressful situation. But the Bible doesn't tell us this, exactly. Instead, we are promised that God will work all things together for our good. It doesn't mean that all things are good, but that God can remodel and restore every situation into something amazing. Have you seen God do this? How have you experienced this truth in your own life? Share an example or a story here.

# YOU HAVE A BEAUTIFUL GIFT

"Flee from sexual immorality. All other sins a person commits are out-side the body, but whoever sins sexually, sins against their own body."

-1 CORINTHIANS 6:18

When I was in the seventh grade, my mentor Susan gave me a beautiful box wrapped in red paper and a large red bow. She told me that there was a red heart inside. This box represented me and my heart. I wasn't to give it away easily or allow anyone to unwrap the box before I was ready. You are also like a beautifully wrapped gift. No one is allowed to have your heart or unwrap your box before you are ready. It's yours to give away. God's best design is that you wait and give your box and your heart away to your future spouse. In this space, draw a picture of your beautiful box. Add a bow. Then, describe what makes your box special—what makes you precious, worthwhile, and adored by God.

# BE REFRESHING

*"A generous person will prosper; whoever refreshes others will be refreshed."*
-PROVERBS 11:25

My friend Deb is incredibly generous and inspiring. She's funny, has a huge laugh, and loves other people. After spending time with her, you just feel better all over. Do you have a friend who makes you feel that way? What are some ways you can bring hope and refreshment to others? Create an action plan. Choose two to three things from this list to be a more generous person to your friends and family. Explain how you will get started.

- ✂ Offer to do a job or chore for a friend or family member.
- ✂ Send an encouraging text to a friend.
- ✂ Offer to pray for someone and actually do it.
- ✂ Call a friend you know is hurting.
- ✂ Reach out to someone who seems lonely.

# RESISTING TEMPTATION

"When tempted, no one should say, 'God is tempting me.' For God cannot be tempted by evil, nor does he tempt anyone; but each person is tempted when they are dragged away by their own evil desire and enticed. Then, after desire has conceived, it gives birth to sin . . ."

-JAMES 1:13–15

I love Cheetos. If given the chance, I could probably eat a whole bag. So I don't buy them anymore. Sinning is a little like eating a bag of Cheetos—it's usually something we like. To avoid sin, we have to stay away from it—like my Cheetos. What temptation pulls at you? Maybe it's a particular food or drink, a certain someone, or a habit. What plans can you put into place to win over this sin? Write down two to three ideas here.

For example, you might:

✕ Ask a good friend to hold you accountable.
✕ Avoid this person or thing as much as possible.
✕ Pray over your temptation and ask God for victory.
✕ Have a mentor you can call when you are tempted.
✕ Memorize a Bible verse that you can go to when you feel like sinning.

# SEEK GOD'S COUNSEL

"If any of you lacks wisdom, you should ask God, who gives generously to all without finding fault, and it will be given to you."

-JAMES 1:5

My daughter needed a job, so she emailed a cute little boutique in the town. Within a few hours, the owner contacted her for an interview, and she was hired. She asked; the door opened. Likewise, the Bible tells us to ask for wisdom when we don't know what else to do—God loves to give it freely and graciously. Write down at least one issue you'd like God's wisdom about. Pray and invite him to show you how to handle this situation.

# BE A LIGHT

"You are the light of the world. A town built on a hill cannot be hidden. Neither do people light a lamp and put it under a bowl. Instead they put it on its stand, and it gives light to everyone in the house. In the same way, let your light shine before others, that they may see your good deeds and glorify your Father in heaven."

-MATTHEW 5:14–16

Last summer, my husband hung these beautiful strings of lights around our backyard. When we turn them on, the whole area shines brightly. Similarly, we are encouraged to be lights in the world. God created us to shine into the darkness and share the light of Jesus with others. Write down two or three ways you can be a light in your community, school, and the world around you. For example: You carry your Bible to school, you are kind to someone you think is hard to love, or you invite the new kid to sit with you at lunch.

# GREAT HABITS TO PURSUE

*"Let us then approach God's throne of grace with confidence, so that we may receive mercy and find grace to help us in our time of need."*

-HEBREWS 4:16

I start every morning the same way: I make a hot cup of coffee, and then I gather up my Bible, devotional book, journal, and pen to enjoy a little time alone with God. I've been doing this since I was 12. (Well, not the coffee.) I still love starting my morning with the Lord because the whole day is better when I do. Do you enjoy time each day in God's presence? Read over the following suggestions, then write down two to three ways you can get more consistent with your devotional time.

- Pick a time—choose a time of day when you will be awake and focused.
- Pick a place—find a place where you can be alone with God.
- Organize your materials—put your Bible, journal, devotional book, and a pen in your place.
- Make a plan—decide how you will spend your time.
- Set your alarm—use your watch or phone as a reminder.

## WEEKLY REFLECTION

During the last seven days we talked a lot about personal struggles, choices, and growth. What area do you struggle most with right now? Why? What can help you overcome and win? Write about these things here. Then, pray and ask God to help you find victory in this struggle.

# INVITE GOD TO BLESS YOU

"Jabez cried out to the God of Israel, 'Oh, that you would bless me and enlarge my territory! Let your hand be with me, and keep me from harm so that I will be free from pain.' And God granted his request."

-1 CHRONICLES 4:10

Today's verse is called the Jabez Prayer. It's a petition—a request for God's help. We can petition God and invite him to do amazing things in our lives. In your own words, write out each portion of the prayer. Then, pray to the Lord.

✗   God, will you bless me greatly today?

✗   Will you enlarge my territory and allow me to have greater influence?

✗   Will you put your hand on my life and give me your favor?

✗   Will you keep me from harm and evil?

✗   Will you free me from pain?

✗   Will you grant my request?

# HEART FRIENDS

"After David had finished talking with Saul, Jonathan became one in spirit with David, and he loved him as himself."

-1 SAMUEL 18:1

Years ago, I met some ladies who taught me the concept of "heart friends." These are friends who deeply love Jesus and deeply love us—no matter what. They are united in spirit, much like the friendship of David and Jonathan in the Bible. Do you know any other Christian girls with whom you are united in spirit? Describe a friend who you believe is a heart friend to you. If you can't think of anyone, invite God to give you a friend like this.

# GIVE THANKS

*"Give thanks to the Lord, for he is good; his love endures forever."*
-PSALM 107:1

God gives us good things all the time, even if we don't always notice them. Think about how God has blessed you. Do you have a warm house, enough food, a supportive parent? Has he helped you work out a problem you've been having? What are you thankful for today? Try to come up with 12 to 15 things you can give thanks for. Tell God how much you appreciate him.

# YOUR IDENTITY IN CHRIST

"But you are a chosen people, a royal priesthood, a holy nation, God's special possession, that you may declare the praises of him who called you out of darkness into his wonderful light."

-1 PETER 2:9

You are extremely precious to God. He absolutely adores you! In him, you have so many incredible gifts. You are chosen. You are royalty. You are holy. You are God's special possession. You have come out of darkness and walk in the light. You are loved. Take a minute to think about how this makes you feel. Complete this sentence: *Because I am so special to God, I feel I can . . .*

# JEALOUSY

"But if you harbor bitter envy and selfish ambition in your hearts, do not boast about it or deny the truth. Such 'wisdom' does not come down from heaven but is earthly, unspiritual, demonic."

-JAMES 3:14–15

My friend Mary was perfect—brilliant, funny, beautiful, and well-liked by all of our middle school friends. Sometimes, it was hard not to be jealous of her. But I soon realized that I had special gifts and talents, as well. I would never be like Mary . . . because God had other plans for me. Perhaps you also find yourself feeling envious of someone. Take a few minutes and pray about those feelings today. Detail your thoughts and ask God to help you let go of the jealousy and focus instead on the incredible plans he has for your life.

# BE QUICK TO LISTEN

"My dear brothers and sisters, take note of this: Everyone should
be quick to listen, slow to speak and slow to become angry."

-JAMES 1:19

Which is easier for you—talking or listening? You may have a big personality
and love to talk and laugh with others. Or you may be introverted and shy, more
of a listener. Did you know that the Bible teaches us all to be quick to listen and
slow to speak? Choose one of these responses and write about what it
means to you.

- ✕  I am slow to speak and quick to hear.
- ✕  I am in the middle. Sometimes I listen well. Other times I have a
  lot to share.
- ✕  I am loud! I talk first and listen later.

# GOD IS WITH YOU

"I will put my dwelling place among you, and I will not abhor you. I will walk among you and be your God, and you will be my people."

-LEVITICUS 26:11–12

Have you ever looked for signs of God at work in your life? For me, I often sense God speaking through the words of a worship song, a message from my pastor, a podcast, a book, the Bible, or even an encouraging text from a friend. Often, God will use these things to send exactly what I need to hear. Have you ever sensed God speaking to you? Share your experience here.

# WEEKLY REFLECTION

Listening to God and to others, you see how precious you are in God's eyes, and what an amazing plan he has for your life. Take a few minutes to read back over your journal entries from the week. How is God growing you? Write down your responses to this question here, and don't be shy about details. Invite God to keep teaching you.

## WHAT MATTERS MOST

"But Martha was distracted by all the preparations that had to be made. She came to him and asked, 'Lord, don't you care that my sister has left me to do the work by myself? Tell her to help me!' 'Martha, Martha,' the Lord answered, 'you are worried and upset about many things, but few things are needed—or indeed only one. Mary has chosen what is better, and it will not be taken away from her.' "

-LUKE 10:40–42

Martha is really upset in this story. She's been doing most of the hard work, and Mary hasn't really helped. Eventually, Martha goes to Jesus with her frustrations and tells him how she feels. How does Jesus answer her? Why do you suppose Jesus says that Mary has chosen what's best? What does that mean, and how might it apply to your life?

# GROWING UP CHRISTIAN

"In fact, though by this time you ought to be teachers, you need someone to teach you the elementary truths of God's word all over again. You need milk, not solid food! Anyone who lives on milk, being still an infant, is not acquainted with the teaching about righteousness. But solid food is for the mature, who by constant use have trained themselves to distinguish good from evil."

-HEBREWS 5:12–14

Think for a minute about your closest friends, teammates, siblings, and family members. How have these people impacted your life? How have they helped you to grow as a Christian? Come up with a name to complete each sentence.

✗ *One of my favorite Bible teachers is . . .*

✗ *A new Christian I know is . . .*

✗ *A mature Christian I know is . . .*

✗ *Someone who encourages me in my spiritual life is . . .*

✗ Complete this sentence: *If someone were to describe me and my spiritual life, they would probably say . . .*

# GOD IS YOUR STRENGTH

"The Lord is my strength and my shield; my heart trusts in him, and he helps me. My heart leaps for joy, and with my song I praise him. The Lord is the strength of his people, a fortress of salvation for his anointed one."

-PSALM 28:7–8

One of my good friends, Elizabeth, is working to get physically stronger. She lifts weights, does cardio, and eats healthily. Over time, she's building strength and feeling much more energetic. Similarly, God can make us stronger and healthier. As we trust in him, pray, and read the Bible, we become strong in the Lord. Take this True/False assessment to check your spiritual strength.

**T/F** *I spend time praying each day and this strengthens me.*

**T/F** *Time reading the Bible regularly gives me energy.*

**T/F** *My Christian friends strengthen me.*

**T/F** *I am learning to trust God and let him help me.*

In the space here, write a prayer asking God to give you great strength today to do all you need to do.

........................................................................................

........................................................................................

........................................................................................

........................................................................................

........................................................................................

........................................................................................

........................................................................................

........................................................................................

# GIVE YOUR WORRIES TO GOD

"Look at the birds of the air; they do not sow or reap or store away in barns, and yet your heavenly Father feeds them. Are you not much more valuable than they? Can any one of you by worrying add a single hour to your life?"

-MATTHEW 6:26–27

The Bible tells us to look at the birds. They don't worry, and God takes care of them. In the same way, we can trust God to take care of us. Make a list of all the things that worry you today. Your grades? Your family? Your friends? Your recital? The big game? Pray about each one and ask God to ease your anxiety.

# HIS GRACE IS ENOUGH

"But he said to me, 'My grace is sufficient for you, for my power is made perfect in weakness.' Therefore I will boast all the more gladly about my weaknesses, so that Christ's power may rest on me. That is why, for Christ's sake, I delight in weaknesses, in insults, in hardships, in persecutions, in difficulties. For when I am weak, then I am strong."

-2 CORINTHIANS 12:9–10

It was a gorgeous day, and I decided to work out on the back porch. As I was setting up, I realized my computer cord would not reach the outdoor power outlet. I had to find an extension cord so I could plug in and get going. God's grace is like an extension cord. When we fall short and don't have enough power to get through the day, we can add the extension cord of God's grace. He promises that his grace is sufficient . . . enough, complete, and able to empower us. Complete this sentence: *Today, I need God's grace to help me . . .*

## SOMETIMES LIFE IS HARD

"Though the fig tree does not bud and there are no grapes on the vines, though the olive crop fails and the fields produce no food, though there are no sheep in the pen and no cattle in the stalls, yet I will rejoice in the Lord, I will be joyful in God my Savior."

-HABAKKUK 3:17–18

Allie, my niece, was devastated when another player got a position on a team she tried out for. She had worked hard and was so disappointed. Have you ever been really let down by something? Maybe a relationship not working out, a bad grade, or a rejection? In the space below, journal a prayer about a disappointment on your heart. Ask God to give you hope that he can use this for good in your life.

# EXERCISING SELF-CONTROL

"But the fruit of the Spirit is love, joy, peace, forbearance, kindness, goodness, faithfulness, gentleness and self-control. Against such things there is no law."

-GALATIANS 5:22–23

Let's talk about your ability to control yourself, your thoughts, and your actions in any situation. Is there a part of your life where you need more self-control? From the list, choose one area where you could exercise more discipline. Then, list two to three ways you can improve. Invite God to strengthen you in this area.

⚹ What I eat and drink

⚹ My schoolwork

⚹ Exercise and health

⚹ Getting more sleep

⚹ My friendships

⚹ My relationships

⚹ My sport, team, or instrument

⚹ My devotional time with the Lord

Christian comedian and author Erma Bombeck once said, "Worry is like a rocking chair: it gives you something to do but never gets you anywhere." Do you ever sit in that rocking chair? How does worrying take up your time but accomplish little? What are three to four ways you can overcome worry in your life? Share your ideas here.

# FILLED WITH PEACE

"Peace I leave with you; my peace I give you. I do not give to you as the
world gives. Do not let your hearts be troubled and do not be afraid."

-JOHN 14:27

When you think about peace, what comes to mind? A beautiful sunset? Lying out
on the beach? A week with no tests? Jesus promises to give us peace. His peace
calms our troubled hearts and takes away our fears. Where in your life do you
need peace today? Take a few moments and journal your thoughts by completing
this sentence: *I would love to have more peace in my life as I think about . . .*

## THE ARMOR OF GOD

"Therefore put on the full armor of God, so that when the day of evil comes, you may be able to stand your ground, and after you have done everything, to stand. Stand firm then, with the belt of truth buckled around your waist, with the breastplate of righteousness in place and with your feet fitted with the readiness that comes from the gospel of peace. In addition to all this, take up the shield of faith, with which you can extinguish all the flaming arrows of the evil one. Take the helmet of salvation and the sword of the Spirit, which is the word of God."

-EPHESIANS 6:13–17

These verses describe the armor of God, which we are called to put on every day. In the space provided, draw a picture of yourself dressed in this armor. Label each piece. Then, decide which piece of armor you most need today.

# THE POWER OF MUSIC

*"Lord, you are my God; I will exalt you and praise your name, for in perfect faithfulness you have done wonderful things, things planned long ago."*

-ISAIAH 25:1

Way back when I was a teen, we listened to music on vinyl. One of my friends had a brother with a huge record collection. We'd sneak into his room and listen to Boston, Kansas, and Fleetwood Mac. I still love to hear those old songs come on the radio. What sort of music do you love? There is so much great worship and inspirational music these days. Finish this thought: *My top three favorite inspirational songs are . . .*

# DEALING WITH BULLIES

"Be strong and courageous. Do not be afraid or terrified because of them, for the LORD your God goes with you; he will never leave you nor forsake you."

-DEUTERONOMY 31:6

My friend Anna was bullied at school by a group of girls. They never physically hurt her, but they called her names, teased her, and harassed her. Finally, Anna talked to a teacher and got some help. Bullying is not okay. If you or a friend are dealing with this, you need to get some help. What might you do to stand up to bullying or help a friend who is being mistreated? Share your ideas here.

# TRANSITIONING TO ADULTHOOD

"When I was a child, I talked like a child, I thought like a child, I reasoned like a child. When I became a man, I put the ways of childhood behind me."

-1 CORINTHIANS 13:11

One of my good friends has a son named Landon. He is really tall (six foot seven and growing!) and plays basketball. Every time he grows, his legs and ankles hurt, and sometimes he isn't very steady. Growth of any kind—physical or emotional—can be exciting and challenging all at the same time. You may be growing smarter in your classes or wiser in dealing with others. In this space, share two to three ways that you see yourself growing and becoming more mature. What do you like about these changes? What has been difficult for you?

# THE STORY OF YOUR LIFE

"... being confident of this, that he who began a good work in you
will carry it on to completion until the day of Christ Jesus."

-PHILIPPIANS 1:6

Today, I'd like you to create a timeline sharing the story of your life. Start with
the year you were born and end with today's date. Include some of your life's
highlights: meeting your bestie, starting high school, trying out and making the
team. Note the ways that God has been working in your life, beginning with
your salvation. Once you finish, go back over your story and thank God for all
that he has done. He began his work in you, and he will keep working until you
meet Jesus. He never stops!

# SEEING INTO THE FUTURE

> " 'For I know the plans I have for you,' declares the Lord, 'plans to prosper you and not to harm you, plans to give you hope and a future.' "

-JEREMIAH 29:11

I've loved the promise of this verse since I was 11. God knows the plans that he has for us. He wants to prosper us, give us hope, and make our futures amazing. What are you looking forward to in the future? Write down five hopes, dreams, or goals you have for your future. Pray over each one and ask God to allow it to happen or to give you something even better. To get you started, I've listed a few that I had in middle school. (By the way, they've all happened!)

- ✗ Go to a great college and get a degree in education.
- ✗ Get a teaching job and inspire young minds.
- ✗ Meet a wonderful man, get married, and start a family.
- ✗ Launch a ministry in which I write books and speak to groups of girls and women.

We reflected this past week on the story of your life. As you think about your past, present, and future, have you enjoyed your story so far? What would you like to change? What do you hope will get better? Take a few minutes and write out a prayer telling the Lord how you feel about your story and your life. Then, write out a prayer for your future. You can use this space to journal this prayer.

# RAISE YOUR VOICE

"For the Spirit God gave us does not make us timid, but
gives us power, love and self-discipline."

-2 TIMOTHY 1:7

In high school, my daughter loved a movie called *Raise Your Voice*. The characters are all in music school, finding their particular calling in music. The lyrics from one of the best songs are, "Raise your voice! / Lift it up to heaven! / Raise your voice! / Come on, don't be shy!" Whether you sing or not, you can raise your voice up to heaven. You can soar using your own gifts. What do you need to shout to heaven? Write about it here.

Here are a few ideas to get you thinking:

✕ Try out for the school play.
✕ Write that book or start that blog.
✕ Launch a podcast or YouTube channel.

## MAKE A DIFFERENCE

"Now may the God of peace, who through the blood of the eternal covenant brought back from the dead our Lord Jesus, that great Shepherd of the sheep, equip you with everything good for doing his will, and may he work in us what is pleasing to him, through Jesus Christ, to whom be glory for ever and ever. Amen."

-HEBREWS 13:20–21

One of my favorite youth pastors likes to ask the teens in our church what they are doing to make a dent in this planet for God. I'd like you to think about this more. What are you doing to make a difference? What are you doing for the Lord that impacts others: taking a mission trip, working in a soup kitchen, making encouraging posts on social media? List two to three ways you can do more good and impact the world around you.

# FOCUS ON TODAY

"Do not boast about tomorrow, for you do not know what a day may bring."
-PROVERBS 27:1

There's an old song called "One Day at a Time" that people used to sing in church. I'd like you to take this idea and break it down further: one project at a time, one class at a time, and one thing at a time. As you go about your day, ask God for the grace to take on one item at a time. Complete a task, then move to the next one. Don't worry about later or tomorrow. In this space, write a prayer asking God for the strength to focus on doing the next right thing all day long.

# FINAL REFLECTION

You've reached the last day of your journey in the *Live in Light* companion journal!

What an adventure it has been. As we've woven our way through the pages of the Bible, we've talked about everything from friends and relationships to anxiety, to your future and your dreams. You've drawn pictures, written out prayers, made lists, taken assessments, and shared your heart.

Now that you are at the end of your trek, take a few moments and look back through the journal. Read over some of your entries. Consider your ideas and thoughts.

Then, answer the following questions here.

✕ What was your favorite devotional? Why?
✕ What was the most meaningful journal day to you? Why?
✕ Did you learn anything new? Interesting? Unexpected?
✕ What will you take with you from your experience with this book?
✕ Is there anything else you'd like to share?

I would love to hear from you. You can share your thoughts and feedback with me on Instagram @melaniemredd, or you can email me at hope@melanieredd.com.

# REFERENCES

Artful Askers. "Wit from Adrian Rogers." Artfulaskers.com/page
/page/4718398.htm.

Goodreads.com. "Albert Einstein Quotes." Goodreads.com/quotes/157357
-the-woman-who-follows-the-crowd-will-usually-go-no.

Goodreads.com. "C.S. Lewis Quotes." Goodreads.com/quotes/10554
-friendship-is-born-at-the-moment-when-one-man.

Goodreads.com. "Erma Bombeck Quotes." Goodreads.com/quotes/140315-worr
y-is-like-a-rocking-chair-it-gives-you-something.

Goodreads.com. "Jim Stovall Quotes." Goodreads.com/quotes/203917
-integrity-is-doing-the-right-thing-even-if-nobody-is.

Integrative Medicine Center of Western Colorado (IMC). "A Joyful Heart is
Good Medicine." Accessed October 30, 2020. Imcwc.com/html5
-blank/a-joyful-heart-is-good-medicine/.

Paris, Melody. "What's In Your Wallet?" CTK Community Church. May 1,
2017. Ctknampa.org/leaders-corner/whats-in-your-wallet.

Peterson, Eugene H. *The Message.* Colorado Springs, CO: NavPress, 2004.

Redd, Melanie. *Live in Light: 5-Minute Devotions for Teen Girls.* Emeryville,
CA: Althea Press, 2019.

## ACKNOWLEDGMENTS

Special thanks to everyone who helped on this project! Thanks to my family for your wonderful support and encouragement. Thank you to my friends who prayed and spurred me on to complete this book. And very special thanks to the amazing team at Callisto—Joe Cho, Wesley Chiu, Carolyn Abate, Mariah Gumpert, and everyone else who made this project soar.

## ABOUT THE AUTHOR

**Melanie Redd** is a Christian blogger, motivational speaker, author, and health coach. She's written five books, including *Live in Light: 5-Minute Devotions for Teen Girls*. She's been married to her husband, Randy, for the past 30 years, and she serves alongside him in ministry. She's also mom to two awesome young adults—a boy and a girl. God's grace never ceases to amaze her. You can find out more about Melanie and her ministry at MelanieRedd.com.